SUPER**SCIENCE**
INFOGRAPHICS

# NATURAL DISASTERS THROUGH INFOGRAPHICS

Nadia Higgins

graphics by
Alex Sciuto

Lerner Publications Company
Minneapolis

Lerner Publications Company
A division of Lerner Publishing Group, Inc.
241 First Avenue North
Minneapolis, MN U.S.A. 55401

Website address: www.lernerbooks.com

Main text set in Univers LT Std 12/15.
Typeface provided by Adobe Systems.

Library of Congress Cataloging-in-Publication Data
Higgins, Nadia.
      Natural disasters through infographics / by Nadia Higgins ;
illustrated by Alex Sciuto
         p.   cm. — (Super science infographics)
      Includes index.
      ISBN 978–1–4677–1287–3 (lib. bdg. : alk. paper)
      ISBN 978–1–4677–1788–5 (eBook)
      1. Natural disasters—Juvenile literature.  I. Sciuto, Alex,
illustrator  II. Title.
      GB5019.H54 2014
      363.34—dc23                                    2013006928

Manufactured in the United States of America
1 – BP – 7/15/13

# CONTENTS

*Introduction*

# LIFESAVING CURIOSITY

Do you have a future in dealing with Earth's big disasters? To find out, take this test.

1. **Have you ever been fascinated by footage of a tsunami that demolishes everything in its path?**

2. **Do you like working with cutting-edge scientific instruments?**

3. **Do you think up creative ways to solve problems and improve things?**

4. **Are you cool with working around volcanoes and melted rock that's more than 1,300°F (700°C)?**

**Did you answer yes to any of those questions?**

## CONGRATULATIONS!

You could have a front-row seat for some of Earth's most exciting and terrifying events. As much as they scare us, natural disasters also mesmerize us. We marvel at their unpredictability, sheer power, and total indifference to human lives. As a scientist, you could be helping to understand them, predict them, and prepare for them.

Scientists cram their curious brains with lifesaving info about Earth's volcanoes, earthquakes, and tsunamis. And they use infographics to help keep that info clear, organized, and easy to remember. Are you ready to see what infographics can do for your own curious brain? Let's get started!

# JIGSAW PUZZLE PLANET!

As a citizen of Earth, you're never really at a standstill. Of course, the whole globe is spinning and zipping through space. But the ground under your feet is moving too. Earth's surface is broken up into seven huge pieces and dozens of smaller ones. These are called tectonic plates. They slide around on a layer of hot, gooey rock.

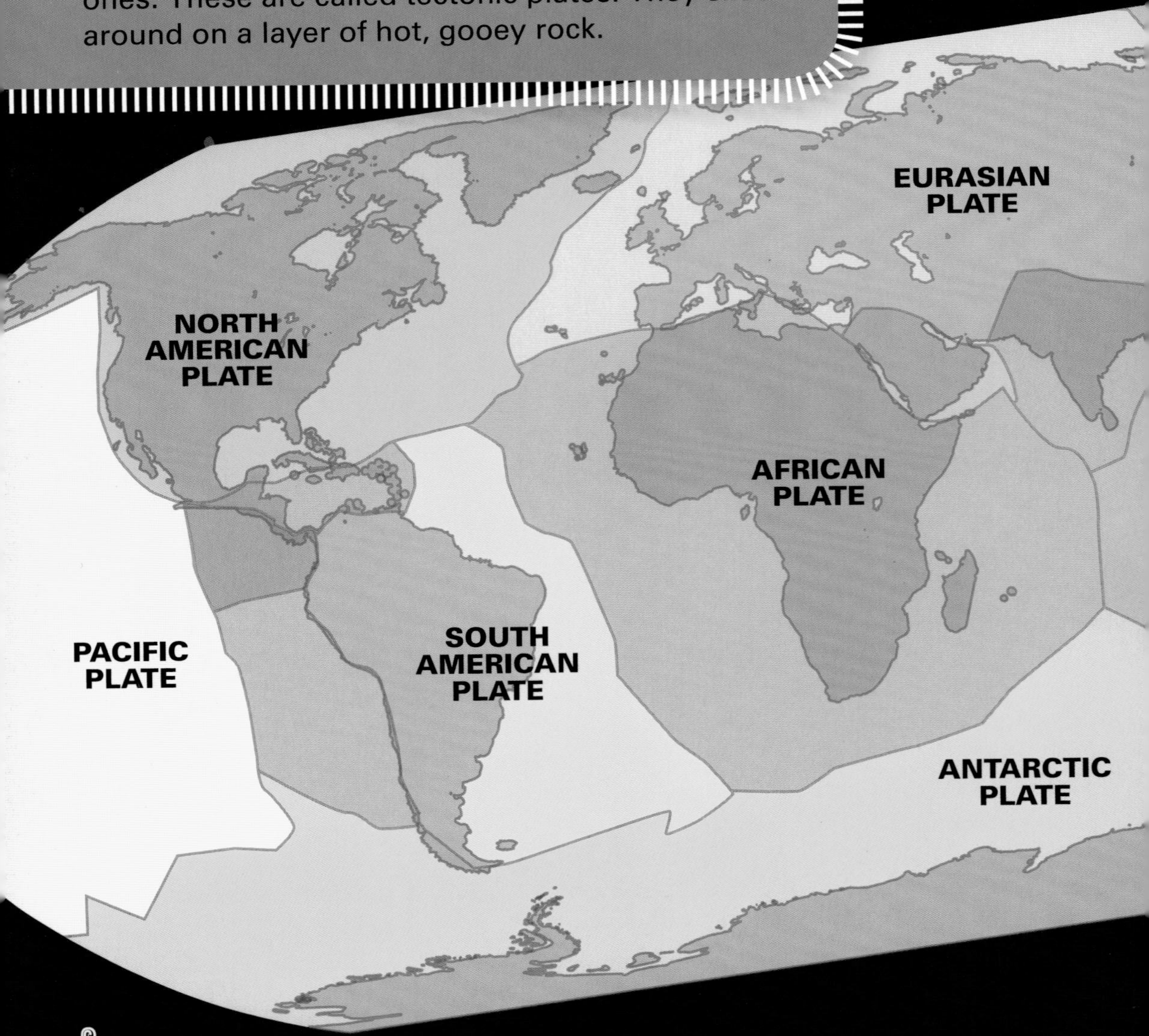

**EURASIAN PLATE**

**NORTH AMERICAN PLATE**

**AFRICAN PLATE**

**PACIFIC PLATE**

**SOUTH AMERICAN PLATE**

**ANTARCTIC PLATE**

## TECTONIC PLATE
Each plate is made up of a chunk of crust and the very top of the mantle underneath it. Plate sizes range from the size of a small country to bigger than a whole continent.

Tectonic plates move at a rate of about 1 to 4 inches (2.5 to 10 centimeters) a year. That's as fast or faster than fingernails grow! That adds up, though. Check out what Earth looked like more than 200 million years ago. Little by little, movement of the plates pulled the continents apart.

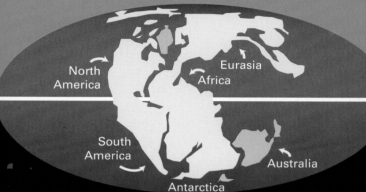

North America

Eurasia

Africa

South America

Antarctica

Australia

**PACIFIC PLATE**

**AUSTRALIAN PLATE**

## CRUST
Earth's rocky shell. It makes up Earth's land as well as the ocean floor.

## 5 to 25 miles
(8 to 40 kilometers)

1,800 miles
(2,900 km)

**OUTER CORE**

1,400 miles
(2,250 km)

**INNER CORE**

400 miles
(645 km)

## MANTLE
This thick layer of superhot rock beneath the crust is melted in spots.

# DRIFT, CRASH, AND GRIND

Tectonic plates are like massive, squirmy puzzle pieces. And where they meet, watch out! Shifting plates cause some of the most spectacular and destructive events on Earth.

Plates interact in three main ways. Each type of plate boundary sets off its own chain of events.

**TRANSFORM BOUNDARY**
Some plates grind past each other. When they get stuck, energy builds up. Then, when they break free, Earth's crust shakes violently.

**EARTHQUAKE**
A sudden shift in Earth's crust makes the ground shake.

## DIVERGENT BOUNDARY

Plates drift apart, and scorching hot magma (melted rock) comes up from the mantle to fill the gap. When the magma cools, new crust is formed. As two plates drift away from each other, they're drifting toward others.

## CONVERGENT BOUNDARY

When plates crash together, the edge of one of the plates goes under the other. The lower edge sinks back into the mantle—and it doesn't always go quietly.

## VOLCANO

Magma, gases, rock shards, and ash come up through an opening in Earth's surface.

## TSUNAMI

A sudden force sets a series of waves in motion out at sea. The waves create a giant wall of water as they near the shore.

# FOUR WAYS TO SPEW

Volcanoes are deadly because of red-hot lava, right? Not exactly. Lava can ruin property and crops, for sure. But you could easily outrun most lava flows. Lahars, or flash floods of hot water and mud, are way more deadly. So are pyroclastic flows. These clouds of hot gases and ash can choke, poison, and burn.

But not all of Earth's volcanoes are to be feared. These magma-spewing spots break down into four main categories, ranging from mild to disastrous.

## SHIELD VOLCANO

Flattest volcano

## FISSURE VOLCANO

Most fun to watch on vacation

### How It's Made
Magma flows up to fill in a gap made by tectonic plates that are moving apart, usually on the ocean floor.

### Eruption
Calm with runny lava and few spewing rocks

### How Often It Erupts
Can be every day

### Example
Mid-Atlantic Ridge

### How It's Made
Runny lava flows quickly from several vents. Lava cools, forming smooth, gentle slopes.

### Eruption
Calm and steady lava flow with few shooting rocks; or bursts of glowing "fire fountains" from the top

### How Often It Erupts
Can be every day

### Example
Mount Kilauea, Hawaii

# THANK YOU, VOLCANOES!

Don't forget to thank volcanoes for the good stuff too, like:

1. *The ground:* A whopping 80 percent of Earth's crust was made by cooled lava from volcanoes.

2. *Rich soil:* Volcano spew is full of nutrients. It breaks down into soil that's awesome for plants.

3. *Clean energy:* People can tap into volcanic energy to make electricity and heat homes.

## CINDER CONE

Most common volcano

## COMPOSITE VOLCANO

Most destructive volcano

### How It's Made
Gravel-sized blobs of lava harden into a simple hill with just one vent. Cinder cone volcanoes are often in clusters on a lava field or coming off the side of a larger volcano.

### Eruption
Somewhat violent; most blasts reach less than 1,000 feet (305 meters) into the air.

### How Often It Erupts
Usually just once

### Example
Paricutín, Mexico

### How It's Made
Layers of cooled lava and other volcanic rock make tall, steep sides.

### Eruption
Very violent with thick, sticky lava; toxic gases; and flying rocks shooting out multiple vents

### How Often It Erupts
Every few hundred years or longer

### Example
Mount Fuji, Japan

# SMALL SHAKES AND BIG SHAKES

Millions of earthquakes ripple through Earth's crust every year. After all, tectonic plates are in constant motion. That sends vibrations, or waves, rippling through the ground. Most of those earthquakes are so small that no one feels them. Others are strong enough to snap bridges, collapse buildings, or even change a river's path.

Scientists use the Richter scale to measure an earthquake's magnitude (M), or strength. A jump of just one number equals 10 times more ground motion—and a 32-fold increase in energy! This graph shows how an earthquake's strength increases sharply with each number.

RICHTER SCALE MAGNITUDE AND STRENGTH OF EARTHQUAKE

## 9.0+

You can actually see waves coursing through the ground.
**Number per year: less than 1**

## 8.0–8.9

Buildings collapse and objects are thrown in the air.
**Number per year: 1**

## 7.0–7.9

A building could slide off its foundation. Railroad tracks bend, and landslides are triggered. **Number per year: 15**

## 6.0–6.9

Walls in well-built houses could crack.
**Number per year: 134**

## 5.0–5.9

You might fall over.
**Number per year: 1,319**

## 4.0–4.9

Stuff slides off shelves.
**Number per year: 13,000**

## 3.0–3.9

It feels like a big truck is rumbling down the street.
**Number per year: 130,000**

## 2.0–2.9

Hanging objects will swing.
**Number per year: 1,300,000**

## 0.0–1.9

It can be detected only by scientific instruments.

# A SERIES OF WAVES

Any sudden disturbance in ocean waters can cause a tsunami. Most often, an earthquake is the cause. But on ancient Earth, crashing meteorites also created tsunami waves.

Tsunamis arrive onshore with little warning. Often the water is suddenly sucked back, exposing the ocean floor. About five minutes later, a wall of water thrashes the shore. It can be as tall as a building several stories high and powerful enough to flip a car.

**2** In deep water, the waves are flat and spread out. Still, they contain enormous amounts of energy.

**3** Waves race toward shore at the speed of a jet plane. Unlike regular waves, these don't break.

**1** An earthquake rocks the ocean floor. A column of water rises. Waves spread out in all directions.

**4** The bottoms of the waves rub against the rising ocean floor. The waves slow down and grow taller and taller.

**5** The first wave crashes onto shore. Then it flows back out—dragging everything with it. Often, several more waves follow, 10 to 60 minutes apart.

# IN THEIR OWN WORDS

On March 11, 2011, a powerful tsunami ravaged the shores of Japan. What was it like for people who were there?

"A mass of pitch-black water was writhing like a living thing."
—Akiko Iwasaki, hotel owner

"When it hit me, it felt like a huge gravitational pull. I couldn't move. I was struggling for breath."
—Tetsuya Tadano, student

"I was in the middle of the street with three customers in my car, and we climbed onto the roof together when the water started coming in."
—Yuichi Kowata, taxi driver

# DANGER ZONES

When it comes to Earth's disasters, the big question is when, not where. Scientists may not know exactly when a volcano will blow or a quake will shake (though they are getting better at predicting). But they do have a good idea of where those events will take place—almost always along the borders of those squirmy tectonic plates.

Regions with many earthquakes

Regions with many volcanoes

About 5 percent of volcanoes form in hot spots rather at than plate boundaries. Here, the mantle is so hot that columns of magma bubble up through the middle of a plate.

The Ring of Fire borders the Pacific Ocean. Here, the plate under the Pacific Ocean is sinking under a continental (land) plate. About 90 percent of volcanoes and earthquakes happen in this zone—causing 80 percent of tsunamis.

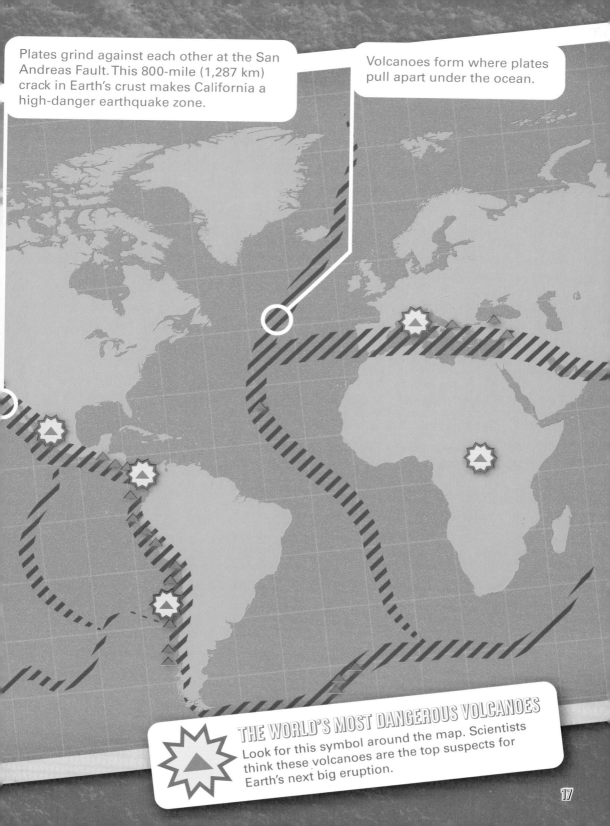

Plates grind against each other at the San Andreas Fault. This 800-mile (1,287 km) crack in Earth's crust makes California a high-danger earthquake zone.

Volcanoes form where plates pull apart under the ocean.

## THE WORLD'S MOST DANGEROUS VOLCANOES

Look for this symbol around the map. Scientists think these volcanoes are the top suspects for Earth's next big eruption.

# RECORD BREAKERS

Check out some of the most amazing volcanoes, earthquakes, and tsunamis of all time.

## Volcano

## Earthquake

### Biggest

**MAUNA LOA, HAWAII**
This shield volcano rises 56,000 feet (17,000 m) from the ocean floor.

**CHILE, 1960**
This quake holds the record for the highest-recorded magnitude—a whopping 9.5.

### Freakiest

**VESUVIUS, ITALY, 79CE**
Volcanic ash completely buried the Roman village of Pompeii, but it also preserved it. Hundreds of years later, archaeologists found whole loaves of bread inside ancient ovens.

**SAN FRANCISCO, 1906**
This earthquake triggered fires that raged for three days. By the end, 28,000 buildings were gone, and more than half of the city was homeless.

### Deadliest

**TAMBORA, INDONESIA, 1815**
This eruption killed 92,000 people. Pyroclastic flows killed thousands instantly. Globally, many more died of disease and starvation as crops failed because of particles in the atmosphere.

**SHAANXI, CHINA, 1556**
Some 830,000 people perished as their dug-out homes collapsed.

# Tsunami

### ISHIGAKI ISLAND, JAPAN, 1971

The tallest tsunami on record came in at 278 feet (85 m) but caused remarkably little damage.

On the map: MAUNA LOA, SAN FRANCISCO, OCEAN ASTEROID ?, CHILE, MOUNT VESUVIUS, SHAANXI, CHINA, ISHIGAKI ISLAND, INDIAN OCEAN, TAMBORA

### ASTEROID STRIKE, 3.5 BILLION YEARS AGO

A giant space rock may have crashed into an ancient ocean. That sent huge tsunami waves racing around the globe several times over.

### INDIAN OCEAN, 2004

Tsunami waves from a 9.0 quake caught Southeast Asia completely by surprise, resulting in 280,000 deaths.

You would have to stack forty-six 6-foot-tall (1.8 m) people to equal the height of the tsunami that hit Ishigaki Island.

6 feet

Math people everywhere agree: sometimes the best way to tell a story is through numbers. Check it out.

# 2,282°F (1,250°

**Temperature of the hottest lava ever measured from a volcano**

# 10,000

**Average number of people who die every year as a result of earthquakes**

# 80

**Number of U.S. volcano that have erupted at lea: once in the past 500 yea**

# 10 to 30

**Average number of seconds an earthquake lasts**

# 9 mph (14 k

**Speed of fastest earthquake vibrations traveling through Earth's crust**

# 260,000

**Estimated number of people killed by volcanoes in past 300 years**

**3 miles** (5 km)

How far ocean water traveled inland during the Japanese tsunami of 2011

**6 mph** (10 kph)

Top speed of most lava flows

**500 mph** (800 kph)

Top speed of tsunami waves

**80**

Percent of volcanic eruptions that happen under ocean water

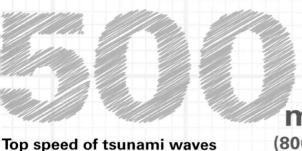

**30 feet** (9 m) Height of Indian Ocean tsunami, 2004

**1,500**

Number of volcanoes on Earth that scientists say could erupt again

**169**

Number of active volcanoes in the United States

Tsunami Center

**$360,000,000,000**

Approximate cost of damage from 2011 Japanese tsunami

Japan

# SURVIVE!

Volcanoes, earthquakes, and tsunamis happen with little, if any, warning. What if the worst happens? Best-case scenario: You and your family have a plan. You've mapped out your evacuation route. You've practiced what to do. Having a few simple steps in your head could save your life when disaster strikes.

## VOLCANO

Local officials will tell you whether to evacuate, where to go, and what routes to take. Meanwhile, take shelter.

**EVACUATION ROUTE**

1. Close all windows, doors, and vents. Turn off heat, fans, and air-conditioning.

2. Put on long sleeves and pants.

3. Go to a room with no windows, if you can—but not the basement.

4. Put a damp cloth over your face.

# TSUNAMI

Sirens, media alerts, and public safety phone messages let you know if a tsunami is on its way.

1. Move inland or to higher ground on foot. You can't afford to get stuck in a traffic jam!

2. Wait for official word before going back to lower ground. Remember, more than one wave could be coming.

# EARTHQUAKE

The key is to protect yourself from falling objects, wherever you are.

## TAKE COVER!

**INSIDE**
Take cover under a table and hold on to its legs.

**IN BED**
Put your pillow over your head.

**OUTSIDE**
Get away from buildings, streetlights, and telephone poles. Get low, and cover your head with your arms.

# JANUARY 12, 2010

One terrible day in 2010, an earthquake took Haiti by surprise. This small Caribbean nation had been struggling with poverty for centuries. Haiti's poorly constructed buildings crumbled. Homes, schools, hospitals, roads, and government buildings lay in ruins.

But the 7.0-magnitude earthquake was just the beginning. Over the following months, the earthquake triggered more problems, even as people around the world reached out to help recovery efforts.

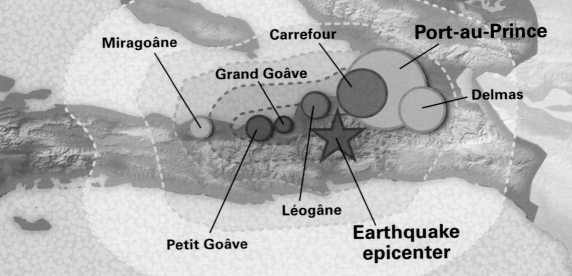

# Haiti

Miragoâne

Carrefour

**Port-au-Prince**

**Grand Goâve**

**Delmas**

Léogâne

**Petit Goâve**

**Earthquake epicenter**

## Map Key

Moderate shaking

Strong shaking

Very strong shaking

Severe shaking

Violent shaking

Extreme shaking

Selected cities and relative population size

# TIMELINE OF EVENTS

**JANUARY 12, 2010, 4:53 P.M.** An earthquake of magnitude 7.0 begins just 15 miles (24 km) from Port-au-Prince, Haiti's crowded capital city. Some 316,000 are killed, and more than 1 million are left homeless.

**JANUARY 15, 2010** The U.S. Air Force opens the Port-au-Prince airport, which has been badly damaged. Desperately needed food, clean water, and medicine start to arrive.

**JANUARY 17, 2010** Looters steal food and supplies amid the chaos in Port-au-Prince. U.S. soldiers arrive to keep peace on the streets.

**JANUARY 20, 2010** Aftershocks continue to rumble daily. A 6.1 magnitude aftershock causes panic in the streets.

**JANUARY 21, 2010** Nine days post-quake, search-and-rescue teams have recovered just 122 people from crumbled buildings.

**OCTOBER 2010** Water and sewage systems are still damaged. Tainted water gives rise to an outbreak of cholera that kills 3,500.

**JANUARY 2011** A full year after the quake, only 5 percent of the rubble has been cleaned up.

**JANUARY 2012** About 70 percent of the rubble has been cleaned up.

**AUGUST, 2012** Some 390,000 Haitians are still living in tent camps under terrible conditions: one shower for every 1,200 people and one toilet for every 77.

**OCTOBER 2012** Protests erupt in the streets. Protesters say the Haitian president is not doing enough to relieve poverty.

**JANUARY 2013** Donor countries have set aside $12.62 billion in aid for Haiti, to be spent by 2020. Safe housing, jobs, and education remain crucial priorities.

Rods inside the panels strengthen every floor.

A wide base tapering to a point makes this building super stable.

Trusses (supports) at the bottom can absorb forces moving both side to side and up and down.

The building rests on a steel-and-concrete block that reaches 52 feet (16 m) deep into the ground. That's deep enough to reach hard soil underneath, which absorbs earthquake waves better than the loose soil on top.

The foundation is designed to move with earthquakes.

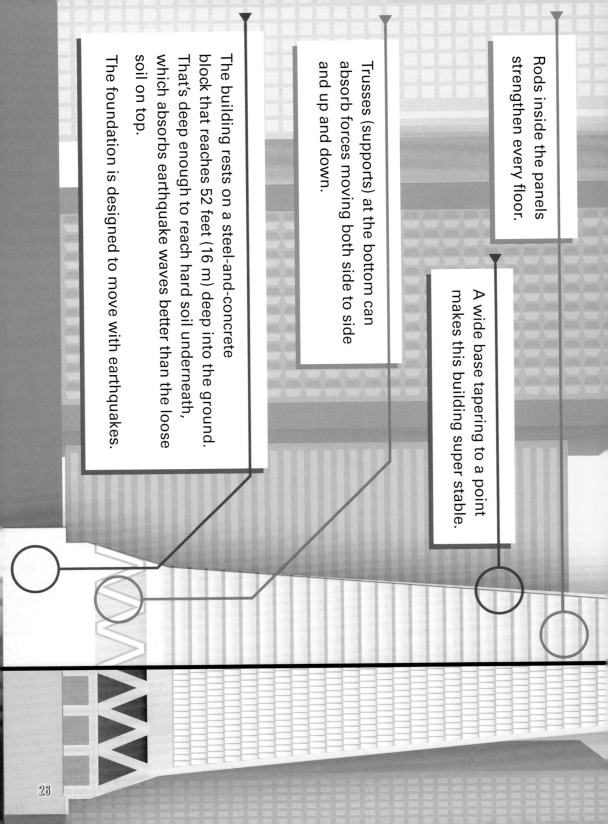

26

# LIFESAVING ENGINEERING

In 1989, a 7.1-magnitude earthquake shook California's Bay Area for more than a minute. In San Francisco, the Transamerica Pyramid's top story swayed almost 1 foot (0.3 cm) back and forth in the sky—as it was supposed to. The city's famous skyscraper was doing exactly what it had been engineered to do, and no damage was done.

Until scientists can better predict quakes, the best way to keep people safe in earthquakes is to reduce damage with earthquake-proof buildings, bridges, and pipelines. Take a look at the lifesaving features of San Francisco's most famous skyscraper.

At 853 feet (260 m), the Transamerica Pyramid is one of the tallest buildings in California. The taller a building, the more flexible it is, so it sways instead of falling.

Spaces between exterior panels allow side-to-side movement.

# SCIENCE SUPERHEROES

Predicting Earth's disasters is so hard, you'd think it must take a superhero. Earthquake signs are unreliable, and many earthquakes seem to come out of the blue. Tsunamis travel so fast that forecasts and warnings need to be made within minutes. And it takes years of studying a volcano's patterns to know when it will blow.

Luckily, superheroes are already in action. Seismologists, tsunami scientists, and volcanologists have saved countless lives with their important work.

## SEISMOLOGIST

**Superpower:** improves ways to detect, locate, and predict earthquakes and reduce the damage they cause

**Cool tool:** seismograph to measure earthquake waves

**Amazing skill:** monitors fault lines where earthquakes are likely to strike

**Heroic feat:** earthquake-proof buildings

**No. 1 goal:** find better ways to predict earthquakes

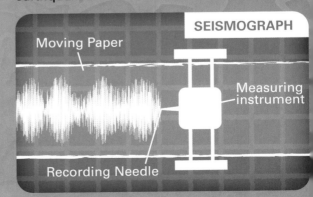

SEISMOGRAPH

Moving Paper

Measuring instrument

Recording Needle

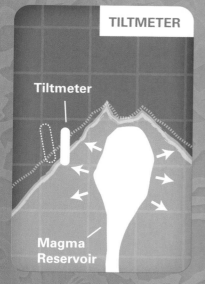

**TILTMETER**

Tiltmeter

Magma Reservoir

# VOLCANOLOGIST

**Superpower:** predicts when volcanoes will blow

**Cool tool:** tiltmeter records the tiniest changes in volcano shape

**Amazing skill:** works on volcanoes while they are erupting

**Heroic feat:** saved an estimated 20,000 lives in 1980 by warning about Mount St. Helens's eruption in Washington State

**No. 1 goal:** better predict size of eruptions, not just when they will happen

# TSUNAMI SCIENTIST

**Superpower:** predicts when a tsunami will happen, how big it will be, and where it will land

**Cool tool:** tsunameter picks up vibrations on ocean floor and relays data to warning centers

**Amazing skill:** can turn raw data into a computerized tsunami model

**Heroic feat:** 70 percent accurate tsunami forecasts

**No. 1 goal:** make that 100 percent

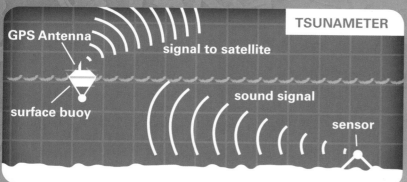

**TSUNAMETER**

GPS Antenna

signal to satellite

surface buoy

sound signal

sensor

# Glossary

**AFTERSHOCK:** a smaller earthquake that takes place shortly after a larger one

**CHOLERA:** an infectious and deadly disease caused by contaminated water

**CINDER CONE:** a small volcano with just one vent. Cinder cones usually erupt just once.

**COMPOSITE VOLCANO:** a volcano with steep sides and infrequent but violent eruptions

**CONVERGENT BOUNDARY:** a place where one tectonic plate slides under another

**CRUST:** the thin, rocky shell that covers Earth, including the ocean floor

**DIVERGENT BOUNDARY:** a place where tectonic plates move away from each other

**FAULT:** a large crack in the rocks that make up Earth's crust. A fault is caused by shifting plates underneath.

**FISSURE VOLCANO:** a type of volcano where magma bubbles up to fill the gap between tectonic plates. Fissure volcanoes are mild and mostly take place under the ocean.

**FORECAST:** to tell when, where, and how a natural disaster will occur

**HOT SPOT:** a place in the middle of a tectonic plate where volcanoes occur

**LAHAR:** a hot, dangerous flow of mud that happens when water mixes with volcanic debris

**LAVA:** hot melted rock that comes out of a volcano

**MAGMA:** hot, melted rock that bubbles up from deep inside Earth. Cooled magma forms much of Earth's crust.

**MANTLE:** the thick layer of hot, partly melted rock below Earth's crust

**PYROCLASTIC FLOW:** clouds of hot gases and rocks that shoot out from a volcano

**RICHTER SCALE:** a numbered scale for measuring the strength of earthquakes based on the size of their vibrations

**RING OF FIRE:** the plate boundary that runs along the edge of the Pacific Ocean. Most volcanoes, earthquakes, and tsunamis occur in the Ring of Fire.

**SHIELD VOLCANO:** a type of volcano with gentle slopes and fast, runny lava. Shield volcanoes erupt frequently.

**TECTONIC PLATE:** one of the massive slabs of rock that fit together to form Earth's crust. Tectonic plates are constantly on the move.

**TRANSFORM BOUNDARY:** a place where two tectonic plates slide past each other. Sometimes they get stuck, building up energy that is released by an earthquake.

Discovery Kids: Volcano Explorer
http://kids.discovery.com/games
/build-play/volcano-explorer
Click around interactive maps, and see what happens inside a volcano. Then try out the cool build-your-own volcano game.

Fradin, Judith, and Dennis Fradin. *Volcano! The Icelandic Eruption of 2010 and Other Hot, Smoky, Fierce, and Fiery Mountains.* Washington, DC: National Geographic Kids, 2010. Check out true life accounts by scientists and everyday people about historic eruptions.

Japan Tsunami: 20 Unforgettable Pictures
http://news.nationalgeographic.com
/news/2011/03/pictures/110315-nuclear
-reactor-japan-tsunami-earthquake
-world-photos-meltdown
*National Geographic* brings you powerful photos from the Japanese tsunami of 2011.

Latta, Sara L. *Lava Scientist: Careers on the Edge of Volcanoes.* Berkeley Heights, NJ: Enslow Publishers, 2009. Learn about what volcano scientists do every day and how you can become one.

*National Geographic*: Forces of Nature
http://environment
.nationalgeographic.com
/environment/natural-disasters
/forces-of-nature/?source=hp_dl
Click on the "lab" tab for cool games and info about earthquakes, volcanoes, and more. Also find maps of danger zones and blow-by-blow stories of the worst record breakers ever.

Ready.gov: Kids
http://www.ready.gov/kids
This U.S. government site offers crossword puzzles, word searches, and other games that teach you how to prepare for the worst.

Storad, Conrad J. *Uncovering Earth's Crust.* Minneapolis: Lerner Publications, 2013. Dig deeper into all the ways Earth's crust shapes your world.

Tarshis, Lauren. *I Survived the San Francisco Earthquake, 1906.* New York: Scholastic, 2012. Curl up with this historical novel about one of the most fascinating natural disasters in U.S. history.

This Dynamic Earth
http://pubs.usgs.gov/gip/dynamic
/dynamic.html
Learn more about plate tectonics from the United States Geological Survey, the nation's government agency in charge of earthquakes and volcanoes.

USGS: Earthquakes Hazards Program
http://earthquake.usgs.gov
/earthquakes/map
Check out this map of earthquakes during the past seven days—literally updated every minute!

# Index

**PHOTO ACKNOWLEDGMENTS**
Additional images in this book are used with the permission of: Wikimedia Commons, p. 18 (left); Pierre St. Amand/NOAA, p. 18 (right); Donald E. Davis/JPL/NASA, p. 19.